DISGUST
DISEASE

BookLife
RAPID
Readers

CONTENTS

Words that look like this are explained in the glossary on page 31.

BookLife
PUBLISHING

©2023
BookLife Publishing Ltd.
King's Lynn, Norfolk
PE30 4LS, UK

Written by:
William Anthony

Edited by:
Hermione Redshaw

Designed by:
Drue Rintoul

PIECES OF THE PAST

Secrets are everywhere. They can be in people's minds or even buried underground. You can find weapons, tools, bodies and buildings just a few metres beneath your feet.

The past is not something you would want to go back to. People had horrible lives and it is easy to see why.

Crime and disaster was happening everywhere.
There was always a war around the corner.
People were often sick or dying, too.
Yet, everyone got on with their lives.

It's time to take a journey into the past. Are
you ready to learn about the hideous history
of gory diseases? It's not for the faint-hearted...

RAT PROBLEMS

In medieval times, towns and cities were much dirtier than they are today. People smelled really bad because they didn't wash. Rats, fleas and lice also spread diseases, including the bubonic <u>plague</u>.

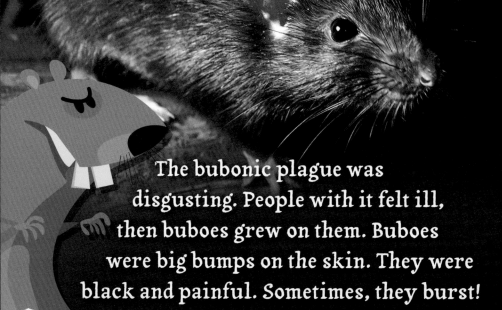

The bubonic plague was disgusting. People with it felt ill, then buboes grew on them. Buboes were big bumps on the skin. They were black and painful. Sometimes, they burst!

Long ago, there were not many hospitals or doctors around. This meant the plague was very deadly. The worst type was called the Black Death.

People think it started in China around 1334. The disease spread around the world. Some <u>historians</u> think between 30 and 60 percent of Europeans were killed by it!

PEOPLE AND POX

Smallpox was one of the deadliest diseases in the world. Yet, this is not just a story about how horrible and scary it was. This is about a human victory, too!

Someone who had smallpox would start getting red spots and sores all over their skin. If the person survived, their lumps would change into scabs and fall off. However, lots of people died.

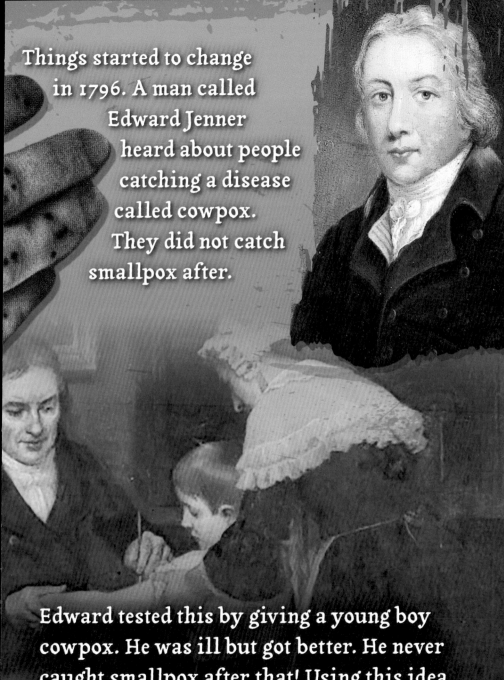

Things started to change in 1796. A man called Edward Jenner heard about people catching a disease called cowpox. They did not catch smallpox after.

Edward tested this by giving a young boy cowpox. He was ill but got better. He never caught smallpox after that! Using this idea, scientists created <u>vaccines</u> that were able to beat smallpox for good!

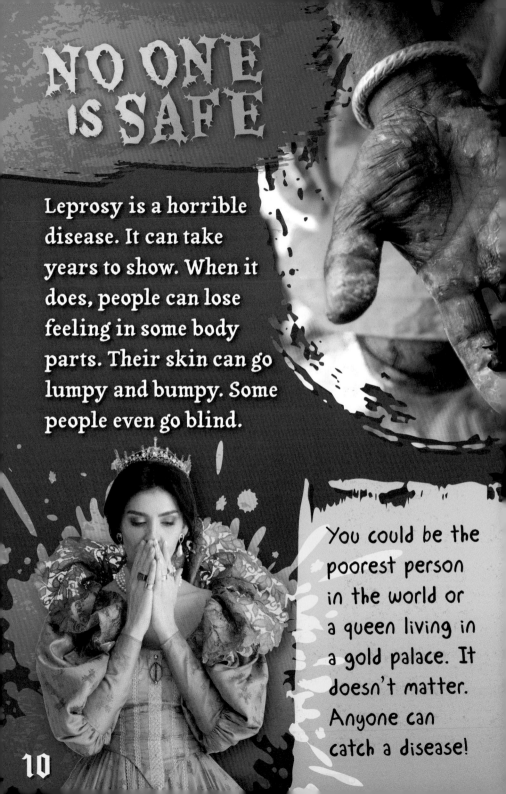

NO ONE IS SAFE

Leprosy is a horrible disease. It can take years to show. When it does, people can lose feeling in some body parts. Their skin can go lumpy and bumpy. Some people even go blind.

You could be the poorest person in the world or a queen living in a gold palace. It doesn't matter. Anyone can catch a disease!

King Baldwin IV found this out the hard way! He had leprosy from a young age. People knew this because he couldn't feel anything in his right arm.

The people loved their king. However, the disease got worse as he got older. Baldwin IV still fought on the battlefield to protect Jerusalem. He won big battles against other armies while fighting against leprosy!

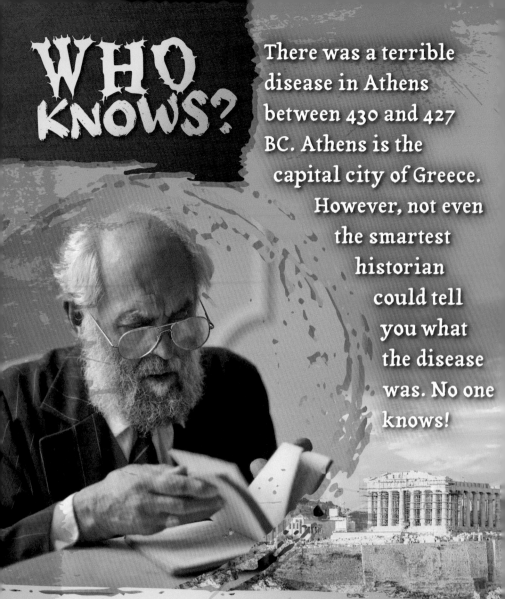

WHO KNOWS?

There was a terrible disease in Athens between 430 and 427 BC. Athens is the capital city of Greece. However, not even the smartest historian could tell you what the disease was. No one knows!

The disease may have killed around 300,000 people. There is not much information about the disease. This is why historians can't tell us what happened.

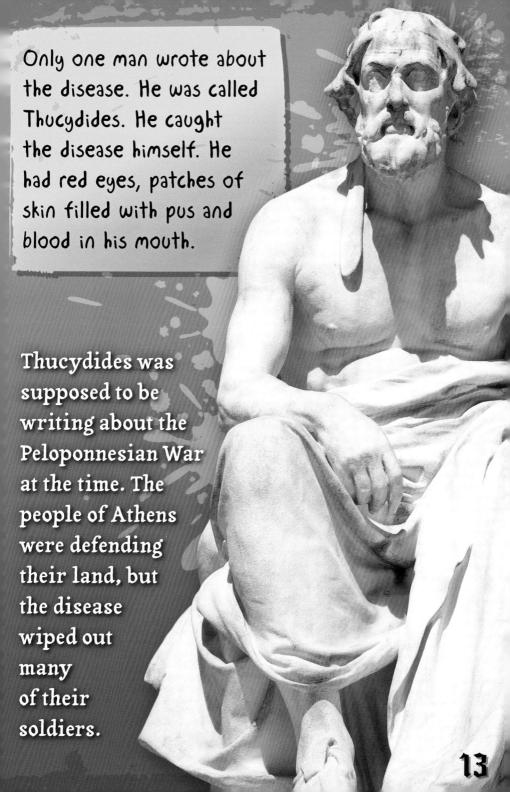

Only one man wrote about the disease. He was called Thucydides. He caught the disease himself. He had red eyes, patches of skin filled with pus and blood in his mouth.

Thucydides was supposed to be writing about the Peloponnesian War at the time. The people of Athens were defending their land, but the disease wiped out many of their soldiers.

QUARANTINE

Being ill today is not the same as it was a long time ago. Today, typhoid fever would give you a headache, a cough and a high <u>temperature</u>.

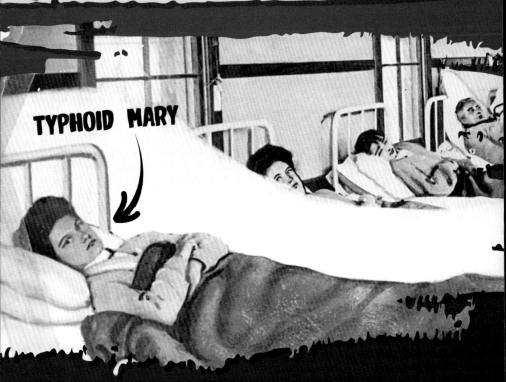

TYPHOID MARY

If you had typhoid fever a long time ago, you would have probably died! A lady nicknamed Typhoid Mary lived in New York over 100 years ago. She had the disease and did not know.

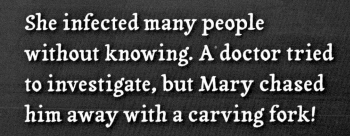

She infected many people without knowing. A doctor tried to investigate, but Mary chased him away with a carving fork!

Mary was eventually caught and taken to a cottage away from everyone. This showed people why it was important to <u>quarantine</u> someone until they are <u>cured</u>. Being quarantined stops deadly diseases spreading.

ARRRRRGH, THAT'S NOT GOOD

Pirates are scary. Pirates with bleeding gums and horrible breath are scarier. If you saw a pirate between the 1400s and 1700s, this is exactly the type of pirate you might meet.

Many of these pirates had a disease called scurvy. People got scurvy when they didn't eat enough foods that have vitamin C.

ORANGES AND LEMONS BOTH HAVE VITAMIN C IN THEM.

People who had scurvy would find their gums bleeding. The skin on their gums would also turn black and their faces would become shrunken.

The only chance they had to get better was to get some vitamin C. However, it was very hard to find fresh fruit while you were out at sea!

DAILY POISON

Most people throughout history agreed on one thing. Lead was great. Lead is a cheap and useful metal.

LEAD TOKENS

People have used it for lots of different things. It can be used in makeup, to make coins and to eat from. There is one problem with lead, though. It is very, very poisonous...

QUEEN ELIZABETH I WORE MAKEUP WITH LEAD IN.

When lead gets into your body, it causes lead poisoning. This gives people pain in their muscles, stomach or head. It also makes people's skin look wrinkly and old.

It would even cause people to lose their minds in really bad cases. Unfortunately, people used it for absolutely everything. As you can probably tell, it didn't end well for lots of people...

TOO MUCH BLOOD

What advice have you been given by your doctor when you have been ill? Have you been told to rest or take some tablets?

If you went to an ancient Roman or Greek doctor, you might have been told something else. They might say you have too much blood in your body! Then, they might offer to let some out...

This is called bloodletting. In the past, bloodletting was used to cure all sorts of things. Even headaches were <u>treated</u> by doing this!

None of this means the idea was right. In fact, it was very, very wrong. Losing blood is usually a very bad thing that can cause people to die.

THE LAST DANCE

One day in 1518, a woman started dancing. There was no music or reason to dance. Her name was Frau Troffea. She lived in a city called Strasbourg, in what is now France.

People laughed and cheered on that first day. However, Frau Troffea didn't stop on the second day. Frau Troffea continued dancing day after day.

By the sixth day, 34 people had joined in. People realised they were dealing with a very strange disease. People danced until they were too tired or died from heart attacks.

Some historians think the dancing disease was caused by eating something that made people <u>hallucinate</u>. No one knows exactly what happened to this day.

23

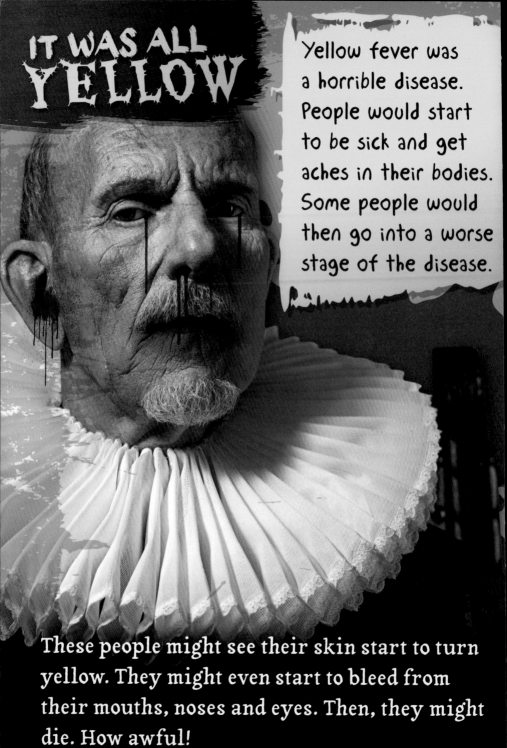

IT WAS ALL YELLOW

Yellow fever was a horrible disease. People would start to be sick and get aches in their bodies. Some people would then go into a worse stage of the disease.

These people might see their skin start to turn yellow. They might even start to bleed from their mouths, noses and eyes. Then, they might die. How awful!

For years, most doctors thought the disease was spread when humans came into contact with each other. They were very wrong.

The cause of the disease was from something very small. Tiny insects called mosquitoes carried the disease. They passed it on to humans by biting their skin.

MOSQUITO

THE DISEASE OF MANY NAMES

Tuberculosis has been around for a long time. Lots of people just call it TB. It has been killing humans for thousand of years. However, it hasn't always had the same name.

In ancient Greece, Hippocrates wrote about a disease that caused lots of coughing and wheezing. He called it phthisis. It was TB all along.

There was a disease called scrofula in the Middle Ages. It was caused by TB. However, people called it 'The King's Evil'. They thought they would get better if the king touched them. They didn't.

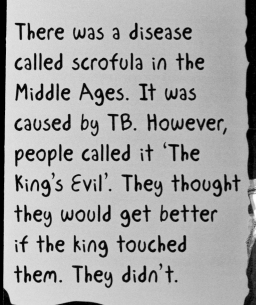

THIS IS A PAINTING OF A CHILD WITH TB.

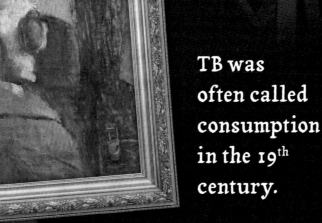

TB was often called consumption in the 19th century.

27

A HOLE IN THE HEAD

How far back in history do you think surgery goes? One type of surgery dates back at least 4,000 years to the Stone Age. It was called trephining.

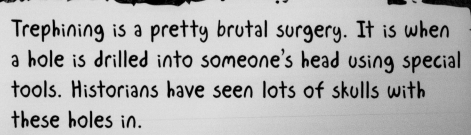

Trephining is a pretty brutal surgery. It is when a hole is drilled into someone's head using special tools. Historians have seen lots of skulls with these holes in.

Many <u>experts</u> think that trephining might have been a way of treating head injuries or getting rid of pain. Other experts think it might have been to treat diseases of the mind.

People at the time might have done it to release evil spirits in someone's mind. No one knows for sure why it was done!

It's OK, you can stop covering your eyes now. Let your breathing slow down. The past was a gruesome place to be, but you are not living there now.

Lots of people in the past met a frightening end. Their horrible stories showed that no matter who you are, no one is safe from disease!

GLOSSARY

CURED to have got rid of an illness completely

EXPERTS people who have special skills or knowledge about a particular subject

HALLUCINATE to see or sense something or someone that is not really there

HISTORIANS people who find out about what happened in the past

PLAGUE a disease that causes death and that spreads quickly to a large number of people

QUARANTINE to keep away from other people to stop the spread of an illness or disease

TEMPERATURE how hot or cold something is

TREATED given medical care and help

VACCINES things that are usually injected into a person to protect them against a particular disease

INDEX

AN INTRODUCTION TO BOOKLIFE RAPID READERS...

Packed full of gripping topics and twisted tales, BookLife Rapid Readers are perfect for older children looking to propel their reading up to top speed. With three levels based on our planet's fastest animals, children will be able to find the perfect point from which to accelerate their reading journey. From the spooky to the silly, these roaring reads will turn every child at every reading level into a prolific page-turner!

CHEETAH

The fastest animals on land, cheetahs will be taking their first strides as they race to top speed.

MARLIN

The fastest animals under water, marlins will be blasting through their journey.

FALCON

The fastest animals in the air, falcons will be flying at top speed as they tear through the skies.